FARM ANIMALS

CONTENTS

What is a Farm?	6
Animals at the Farm	8
Cows	10
Cow Breeds	12
Buffaloes	14
Oxen	16
Horses	18
Goats	20
Donkeys and Mules	22
Sheep	24
Pigs	26
Dogs	28
Chickens	30
Turkeys	32
Ducks	34
Other Livestock	36
Taking Care	38
Poultry Care	40
Farm Stories	42
Glossary	44
Index	45

WHAT IS A FARM?

A farm is a large area of land that is mainly used to grow crops, and to rear animals like cows, sheep and pigs.

▲ Large farms are used to rear animals all around the world

▲ Dairy farms use specialised equipment to obtain and preserve milk produced by animals

Animal Farms

Not all farms grow crops. Some farms rear animals like cows, pigs, sheep, chickens and other fowl. These are specialised farms and require equipment to handle a large stock of animals, such as tractors. More animals are being bred than ever before, to meet the demands of the world, which means an increase in the production of milk, meat, eggs and other farm animal derived products.

Dairy Farms

Dairy farms breed cows, buffaloes, goats and sheep to produce large quantities of milk and meat. The animals are often fed special nutritious food to increase productivity and meat. In fact, some dairy farms even grow their own feed like corn and hay that the animals eat. Some dairy farms also crossbreed species to produce new species. Dairy farms usually sell off male calves, because they don't produce milk.

Poultry Farms

Poultry farms raise chickens, turkeys, geese, ducks and other fowl. Poultry farms raise these fowl mainly for meat while layer poultry farms raise fowl to produce eggs. Poultry farming is a specialised business. Breeders need to choose the right species to get the desired fowl. So the breeder is able to raise chickens with less or more fat, or ducks that yield more eggs! Though poultry farms mainly produce meat and eggs, they also yield feathers for pillows and quilts.

▲ Poultry farms raise fowl for meat and eggs

ANIMALS AT THE FARM

Many kinds of animals are raised on the farm. These animals are known as livestock. Livestock are bred for food, fibre or labour.

Animals Of All Sorts

Livestock comprises of all animals that are bred at the farm. Cattle are members of the bovine family, some of which are bred for milk and meat while the rest are reared for labour. Animals like horses or bulls are specifically bred at the farm for labour like plowing the field, pulling carts and helping in transportation. These are known as working animals, or 'beasts of burden'. There are also animals like sheep and goats that are bred for their wool as well as meat. However, animals like pigs are specifically bred for meat. The skin and fur of the animal can also be used to make various products. Farm animals are also often traded at auctions.

▼ *Farm animals are at risk from infection and disease if they are kept in unhygienic conditions*

Many Uses

Apart from milk, meat, eggs, fibre, feathers and labour the animals on a farm can also have other uses: livestock dung is a very good organic fertiliser for the field; this improves the quality of the soil and increases productivity. In India cattle dung is used to plaster walls and make dung cakes that are burnt as fuel. However, the farmer must ensure that the dung is carefully stored to prevent the spread of diseases. The grazing of livestock also helps to control the growth of weeds.

▲ Confining large numbers of livestock in small enclosures is not only illegal but also dangerous for their health

Managing livestock

Raising livestock is not an easy job: the farmer needs to know which animals are compatible and can be kept together; they must provide shelter for them; there should be enough space and natural surrounding for the livestock to graze on; the livestock should be guarded and protected by shepherds and watchdogs.

▲ In fire-prone regions of some farms, animals are encouraged to graze on dry scrub to reduce the risk of fire

COWS

Cows are among the most important farm animals.
They provide us with milk, meat and leather. Cows can also
serve as draft animals and help some to plough fields and pull carts.

Farm Friend

Cows belong to the family of bovines which also includes water buffaloes, bisons, yaks and spiral horned antelopes. Cows are among the first animals to be domesticated for agricultural purposes. Cows are quite harmless but if you pester them too much you might get a kick or a butt from their head! Cows are mainly useful for the nutritious milk they give. Their flesh, called beef, is also relished as food by many. Their hide is used as leather to make products like shoes and bags. Since they are quite sturdy and can also be easily trained, in many parts of the world they are often a major helping hand on the farm, carrying loads and ploughing fields.

◄ Cows are the most important dairy animals and are used for a variety of purposes

Food and Shelter

Cows on the farm must be taken care of properly. They should be provided with good shelter and nutritious food. They should be housed in wooden or brick barns or cowsheds. Good food is vital to good health. So cows must be fed juicy grass and hay as a part of their diet. They should also be fed an occasional diet of grain. Cows also like to graze on open pastures. In fact, cattle are often allowed to graze on large patches of grass. This ensures a good use of land that might not be suitable for growing other crops.

▼ *Shelters for cows should be safe, clean and hygienic*

Milking a Cow

Cows provide us with milk. This milk can be used to make various dairy products like cheese, cream, butter and yoghurt. But, for this, cows need to be milked using a proper technique. They should be milked by hand or machines. Milking machines are often used on farms. These machines can extract large quantities of milk and are vital for producing dairy products on a large scale. These milking machines also process the milk in sealed containers. This makes the process more hygienic and also prevents the milk from getting spoilt.

◄ *Extracting milk with the help of machines increases the amount obtained from a cow*

COW BREEDS

The black and white markings on this holstein cow are known as cow spots

There are many different species of cows. The different species are bred selectively to produce desired characteristics like strength, meatiness and ability to yield more milk.

The Aberdeen-angus is the only breed of cow in the world that is reared exclusively for beef

Beefy Aberdeen-angus

Aberdeen-angus is one of the most popular beef breeds. They are very popular in New Zealand, having been imported from Scotland during the early 19th century. They are good-tempered, hardy and undemanding cattle. Aberdeen-angus cattle are also known to breed and calve easily. Raising the cattle is relatively economical compared to other breeds and is thus preferred by many farmers. Aberdeen-angus cattle yield more flesh than most other beef breeds and are therefore more profitable. However, they are not good providers of milk for human consumption. Their beef is quite a favourite with meat lovers as it is tender, juicy and tasty.

Patchy Holstein

The holstein cow originated in the Netherlands and this black-and-white-patched cow is now seen throughout the British countryside. It is a large cow and is extensively used in dairy farming as it yields large quantities of milk. On average a holstein cow can produces 7-8 thousand litres (1.8-2.1 thousand gallons) of milk in a year! The productive life of a holstein cow is between three and six years, yielding about 30 thousand litres (6.5 thousand gallons) of milk!

CREATURE PROFILE

Common Name:	Holstein
Colour:	Black and white patches
Height:	1.5 m (4.9 ft)
Weight:	680 kg (1,500 lbs)
Feed on:	Hay, alfalfa, corn, grass

Small Jersey

The Jersey cow is one of the oldest breeds of dairy cow and one of the most common dairy breeds in the world. It originated on the island of Jersey in the English Channel and is extremely adaptable to different climatic and grazing conditions. It can be found throughout the world, from Europe, to South America, parts of North America and even Southeast Asia. The colour of Jerseys varies from fawn to brown. It can have a solid colour or be splashed with white. It is a smallish, docile cow and quite a favourite with dairy farmers because it requires less space and food, making it quite economical. Moreover, the Jersey can produce 13 times its own body weight in milk! This milk is very rich in butterfat and protein.

▼ *Jersey cows vary widely in colour and can range from light grey to fawn, to an almost black shade in some instances*

BUFFALOES

There are several species of buffaloes. Some live in the wild, but the water buffalo is a tamed variety and is kept at farms throughout the world – most commonly in Asia and America.

Two Types

Water buffalo comprise of two main breeds: the swamp buffalo and the river buffalo. The swamp buffalo is slate grey in colour and has a droopy neck with massive swept back horns. It loves to wallow in mud puddles, especially on hot days. The river buffalo is black or dark grey in colour with tightly curled or drooping straight horns. It prefers wallowing in clean water. Adult water buffaloes of both types stand about 1.8 m (5.9 ft) at the shoulder and stretch up to 2.9 m (9.5 ft) in body length. They weigh between 300 to 600 kg (662-1,322 lbs). Wild water buffaloes are considerably larger and can weigh as much as 900 kg (1,984 lbs). In both cases the male is larger and heavier than the female.

Milk and Meat

Buffaloes yield rich milk in large quantities. A female buffalo can produce about four thousand litres (1,057 gallons) of milk annually! Buffalo milk has double the amount of butterfat than cows milk and is used for the production of cheese and curd. In northern India, the cream from the milk is used to make ghee — an oily substance used in cooking. Buffalo meat is also fast becoming popular because it has less fat and bone and is cheaper than beef in some parts of the world.

▲ Buffaloes spend a lot of time wallowing in water to escape the heat

Cost-efficient Cattle

Buffaloes consume about 1.5-2 per cent of their bodyweight in food everyday. They are also less choosy about their food and will eat a variety of weed and brush that other cattle refuse. The murrah is a premier milking buffalo. It originated in Haryana and Punjab but is now reared in many other countries of the world. It yields large quantities of milk and is also known as the holstein of the buffalo world! The milk of the murrah is the basis of mozzarella cheese production in Italy.

▲ Dairy products like cheese, butter and drinking milk can be obtained from the milk produced by buffaloes

▼ Buffaloes are often used to plough fields in various parts of the world

CREATURE PROFILE

Common Name:	Murrah
Colour:	Jet black
Height at withers:	Male: 1.4 m (4.6 ft)
	Female: 1.3 m (4.2 feet)
Weight:	Male: 550 kg (1,200 lbs)
	Female: 450 kg (990 lbs)
Feed on:	Grass, clover and straw

OXEN

Oxen are bulls that have been castrated and trained to serve as draught animals. They have more stamina than other cattle and are therefore preferred for heavier work.

Intelligent Animals

Oxen are quite intelligent animals and respond to training positively. They are trained from a young age by teamsters or trainers to respond to signals. The teamster gives verbal commands like 'get up' or 'back up', or makes a noise like a whip-crack to train the animal. Since the oxen's performance depends largely on training, they must be at least four years of age before they can begin work properly. The Ayrshire breed of oxen is medium in size and is a popular breed among farmers for its strength.

◀ Oxen are also used to plough agricultural fields in some parts of the world

The Preferred Breed

Oxen are often preferred to horses because they have more endurance; they are less prone to injuries and can pull harder and longer on extremely heavy loads; they are sturdier and extremely hardy animals; moreover, unlike horses, these animals are not choosy about their diet and can even live off grass or sage. This makes them easily adaptable and economical to rear. It is for this reason that they are especially used in developing countries. But these durable animals often go malnourished in poverty stricken regions.

◄ *Oxen have often been used as transport and also to carry material from one place to another*

▼ *Bull trains were used during the great westward migration*

As old as America

Oxen were used extensively as draught animals and for plowing from the time of early settlements in America. Though oxen are rather slow, their strength and endurance make up for it. They were especially useful in carrying logs and heavy loads on rugged muddy roads, where horses failed. They were also used to draw wagons during the great westward migration. Sometimes as many as ten oxen were yoked (tied) together, to pull wagons that were hooked together and drawn over rough trails: these were known as bull trains.

CREATURE PROFILE

Common Name:	Ayrshire cow
Colour:	Red and white patches
Weight:	Adult male: 816–907 kg (1,800–2,000 lbs)
	Adult female: 540–590 kg (1,200–1,300 lbs)
Feed on:	Hay, grass, sage

HORSES

Horses are among the most magnificent and beautiful looking animals. They have a lot of strength and stamina and are very fast runners, making them an asset to many farms.

Draught Horses

Most breeds of horses can carry humans on their backs with ease and can also be harnessed to pull objects. Horses are increasingly being selectively bred for specific jobs: there are lighter horses for racing and heavier ones that are used on farms. Farm horses are known as draught horses. These horses are large, healthy, muscular and powerful. They are also extremely adept at performing hard tasks like ploughing, carrying heavy loads and pulling carts.

Eat Well to Stay Well

Horses are kept in stables on farms, which are safe and comfortable for them. Dirty stables breed diseases and so must be cleaned regularly. As draught horses work very hard they need to be fed adequately. A typical diet comprises of a bulk of roughage like hay and grass and some concentrates like oats and barley, which provide them with energy for heavy physical labour.

▲ Draught horses are used to perform a large number of heavy tasks at the farm

▲ Horses need to be given a complete diet of hay, grass and oats to keep them healthy and fit

CREATURE PROFILE

Common Name:	Suffolk punch
Colour:	Shades ranging from light gold to dark brown
Height:	1.6–1.7 m (5.2–5.7 ft)
Weight:	770–910 kg (1,700–2,000 lbs)
Feed on:	Hay, alfalfa, oat, barley, fresh grass

▲ Shirehorses are used as draught animals as well as for public shows

Many Breeds

There are several breeds of draught horses: Shirehorses are powerfully built, tall animals, standing up to 2 m (6.5 ft) at the shoulder. This breed is believed to have developed from the medieval great horse that was brought to England by William the Conqueror; the Irish draught horse, the national horse of Ireland, is an active and powerful horse. It is an intelligent, gentle and docile animal and easy to work with. It is usually used for hunting and riding and also makes a good competition horse; the Suffolk Punch was developed to plough the heavy clay soil of the counties of Norfolk and Suffolk. Typically chestnut in colour, these horses are popular for their stamina, strength, health and good temperament.

GOATS

Goats were domesticated about 10,000 years ago and continue to be bred in farms across the world. They provide milk, meat, hair and skin.

Nutritious Milk

Like cows, goats are also bred for dairy purposes. The milk can be drunk or processed into cheese. Goats' milk contains less lactose (a type of sugar) than cows' milk so is recommended to those with an intolerance. Unlike cows' milk, goats' milk is naturally homogenised (meaning it stays smooth): this is because it lacks the protein agglutinin.

▶ Goats' milk has comparatively low levels of cholesterol and is extremely rich in phosphorus, calciums and vitamins

Common Name:	Angora goat
Weight:	Male: 82–102 kg (180–225 lbs)
	Female: 32–50 kg (70–110 lbs)
Feed on:	Shrubs, bushes and woody plants

Soft Fleece

Some goats are bred for their fibre. Goats wear two coats of hair: an outer coat, which is coarse and is the longer guard hair, and an inner, softer, fleece coat. The latter is used to make soft wool. The fleece is either sheared or combed. Fleece from goats is much more expensive than sheep wool since goats yield a better quality but a lesser amount of fibre. The fleeces of Angora and Cashmere goats are very famous. They are fine, soft and very warm and often used to make shawls with intricate embroidery.

◄ *Cashmere goats are usually very healthy animals and also require minimal care to raise*

Meat and Hide

The goat is useful both alive and dead. When alive it provides milk and fleece and provides meat and hide when dead. The goat's meat is tender, with low fat content compared to other red meat like beef. It is popular in the Middle East, South Asia, Africa and The West Indies. One of the most popular goats raised for meat is the South African boer. In places like Indonesia goatskin is used to make a native instrumental drum skin named bedug.

► *Both the meat and the skin of the goat are used for various purposes*

DONKEYS AND MULES

In some parts of the world mules and donkeys often serve as beasts of burden on farms. They help in transporting heavy loads from one place to another and are also often ridden.

Donkeys

Donkeys have many uses at the farm. They not only function as beasts of burden helping to pull carts and buggies but also make excellent stable companion for foals and horses because of their generally friendly nature. They can also have a calming effect on nervous horses. The miniature Mediterranean donkey is a unique species and is known for its small size. It originates from the island of Sicily. Because of its size, the Mediterranean was traditionally used to turn grinding stones for grain inside people's houses.

Mules

The mule is the offspring of a male donkey and a female horse. It has the patience, endurance and balance of a donkey and the strength and power of a horse. They are also naturally resistant to diseases that many horses suffer from. Mules are supposedly stubborn. However, it is up to the trainer to earn their confidence and make them work.

▶ *Despite their reputation, Mules are generally very patient and hardworking animals - although they do have a dangerous kick if provoked*

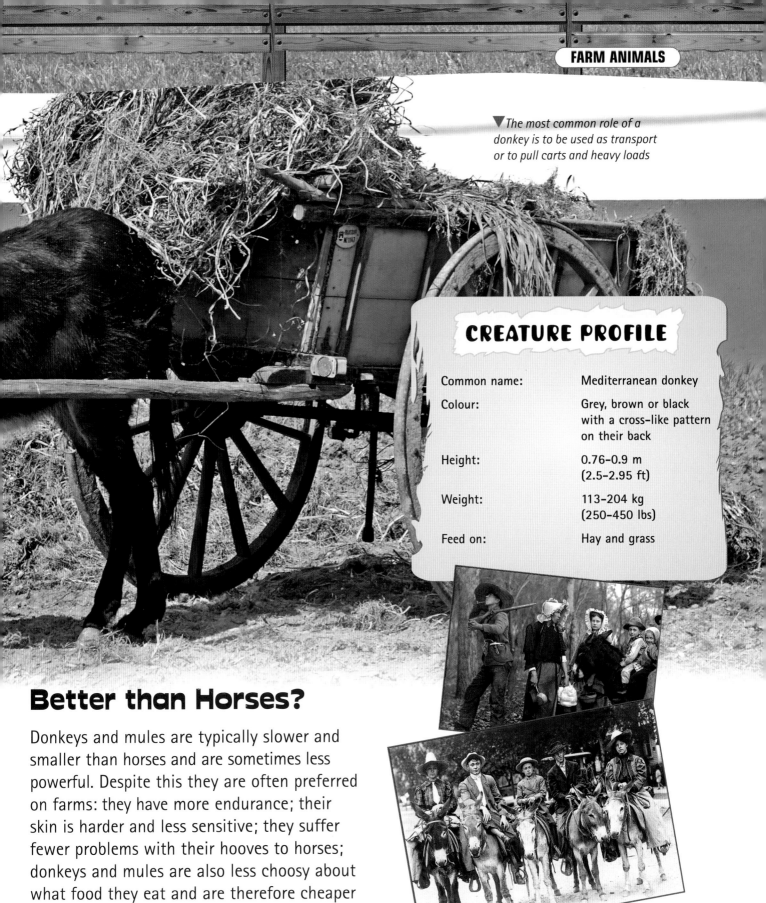

▼ *The most common role of a donkey is to be used as transport or to pull carts and heavy loads*

CREATURE PROFILE

Common name:	Mediterranean donkey
Colour:	Grey, brown or black with a cross-like pattern on their back
Height:	0.76–0.9 m (2.5–2.95 ft)
Weight:	113–204 kg (250–450 lbs)
Feed on:	Hay and grass

Better than Horses?

Donkeys and mules are typically slower and smaller than horses and are sometimes less powerful. Despite this they are often preferred on farms: they have more endurance; their skin is harder and less sensitive; they suffer fewer problems with their hooves to horses; donkeys and mules are also less choosy about what food they eat and are therefore cheaper to feed; because of their hardiness these animals usually require less care and maintenance than horses.

▲ *Donkeys have been used as a mode of transport for many years*

SHEEP

**Sheep are peaceful animals that can be easily tamed.
Man domesticated sheep over 10,000 years ago.
Sheep yield wool, sheepskin, excellent meat and even milk.**

Sheep Farming

Sheep farming, also known as sheep husbandry, is the raising of sheep for various products. Lambs, or young sheep, are raised for their tender meat while the adults provide us with wool. Some sheep are even raised for milk. Sheep are kept in flocks or a group in pens or barns. They are grazers and need enough field or paddock to graze on. But farmers have to ensure that the paddock is fenced to prevent sheep from wandering away. Coyotes, foxes and wild dogs pose a threat to sheep, particularly newborn lambs. In the case of larger flocks, shepherds and sheep dogs are used to look after and protect the flock.

Warm Wool

Shearing is the process by which the woollen fleece of a sheep is removed. A sheep is typically sheared once a year. The shearer traditionally used a blade shear, but now a machine shear is used for speed and ease of use. Skilled shearers take great pride in the number and quality of fleeces they can shear in a day. In some parts of the world they even hold competitions where shearers compete to prove who is the best!

◄ *A sheep is sheared using traditional blade shears*

CREATURE PROFILE

Common Name:	Southdown sheep
Colour:	Cream, beige and grey with black face and legs
Weight:	Male: 86–104 kg (190–230 lbs)
	Female: 59–81 kg (130–180 lbs)
Feed on:	Hay, legumes, alfalfa

▲ *Sheep need large patches of fresh grass to graze on*

Different Breeds

Different breeds of sheep are bred for different purposes. Some yield more wool, some yield more meat, while some female sheep produce more lambs in a year and some others are fast growing. The southdown breed is one of the woolliest sheep breeds of the UK. It yields wool of fine texture and thickness. The Suffolk breed is one of the most dominant mutton sheep breeds in the world, while the east friesian is the most milk productive: it gives between 300-600 litres (80-160 gallons) of milk per year!

▶ *The Southdown sheep is known for good lambing ability and produces average quantities of milk*

PIGS

Pigs are also known as hogs or swine. Domestic pigs are usually pink or brown with hair on their bodies. They are bred for their meat.

Pens and Piggeries

Piggeries are animal farms that specialise in rearing domestic pigs for commercial use. In this system of pig production, mature pigs are kept indoors in sheds while pregnant female pigs, also known as sows, are kept in separate stalls. Breeding pigs in piggeries improves the general condition of the pigs. Pigs do not have sweat glands, so most breeds are at risk from heatstroke in hot temperatures. Piggeries control the temperature through ventilation and drip water systems. Pigs produce a lot of waste so it is important that they are frequently mucked-out.

CREATURE PROFILE

Common name:	Domestic pig
Colour:	Mainly brown and black
Weight:	100 kg (220 lbs)
Feed on:	Plants, fungi, roots, grain and berries

▼ Pigs are usually housed together in piggeries

Domestic Pig

The domestic pig is a descendant the wild pig but has a milder temperament. The domestic pig is a pack animal and is usually kept in large groups of 10 animals. The sows are usually more aggressive than the male pigs or boars and are kept separate. The domestic pig is one of the most popular breeds to be reared commercially because its meat is more tender and has a higher fat content than other breeds. Other than for its meat, the domestic pig is also used for its skin and intestines. Even the hair on its skin can be used to make brushes.

▲ The domestic pig is reared mainly for its meat, known as pork

England's Own

The large black pig, known as the Devon pig, is the only black pig found in Britain. Originally bred in Devon, these pigs have a shorter body and stronger bones than other breeds. The dark coloured coat makes this breed extremely hardy and also helps prevent skin diseases more common in other pigs. This hardy species also yields good quantity of meat and excellent milk.

▼ Large black pigs, or Devon pigs, are also known for the superior quality of milk that they produce

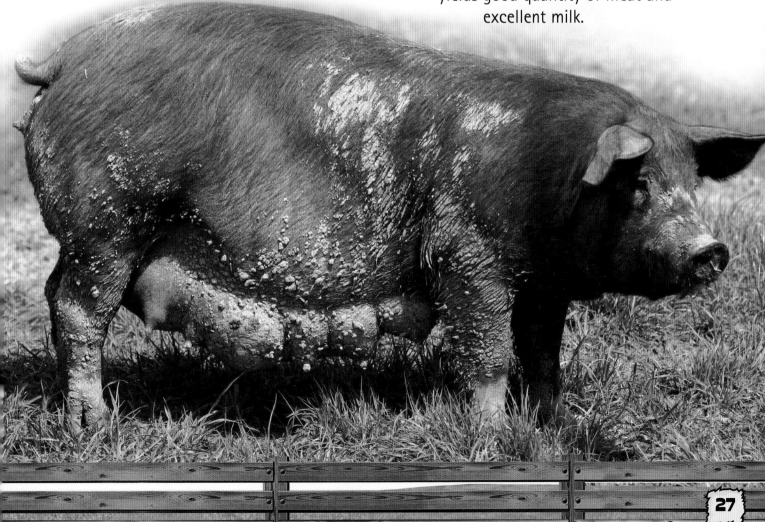

DOGS

Some breeds of dog are specially
trained for herding animals on
farms. Indeed, dogs are a common
sight on many farms.

Styles of Work

Herding dogs have physical characteristics like speed and
endurance that help them to work. They are used to
protect farm animals from wild animals and other threats.
Although most commonly used to herd sheep, dogs are
sometimes used to control cattle, goats and even poultry,
by moving them to the desired spot. Herding dogs are
highly trained and responsive to their master's instruction.
Signals and commands are usually given in the form of
whistles and shouts - each one prompting the dog to act
in a different way towards the herd.

▶ The Australian cattle dog
is a muscular and strong animal

▲ *Grazing sheep are watched closely by the border collie*

CREATURE PROFILE

Common Name:	Border collie
Colour:	Mainly black with white patches
Height:	0.4–0.5 m (1.3–1.6 ft)
Weight:	14–23 kg (30–50 lbs)
Feed on:	Ideally, low-fat, high protein meat and biscuits

Australian Cattle Dog

The Australian cattle dog is also known as the Queensland heeler. This medium-sized dog was instrumental in building the cattle industry of Australia. It is alert, courageous and hardy. It is also very cautious by nature. This dog is a nipping dog (meaning it chases the heels of the herd) and is used to move cattle. It is an active breed with excellent stamina and is happiest when involved in some kind of activity or exercise.

▶ *A border collie prepares to 'come by' - an instruction given to it by the herder*

Border Collie

The border collie is a popular farm dog. Bred originally in Great Britain, it is regarded as one of the most intelligent farm dogs. It is a quick learner and understands human directions well. It is obedient and therefore makes a good farm dog. With its great energy, agility and herding instincts it can manage many kinds of animals — from sheep and cattle to poultry. This dog is a header dog, meaning it will run ahead (and around) the herd in order to affect its movements.

CHICKENS

Chickens are the most common and widespread domesticated animal in the world. They are usually mass-bred for meat and to produce eggs, but are also commonly kept as pets in some parts of the world.

Cluck Cluck!

Male chickens are known as roosters while female chickens are called hens. Chickens are gregarious (social) birds and live in large flocks. Chickens like to lay eggs in nests that already contain eggs - something that is often encouraged by farmers with the placing of fake eggs. Domestic chickens cannot fly long distances, but those raised in open-air farms generally have the feathers of one of their wings clipped to prevent them from flying over boundary fences.

Cornish Hens

The Cornish hen is widely bred for the poultry meat industry. They were first bred in the county of Cornwall in England and were known for their large amount of white meat and smooth and fine texture. They have short feathers, stuck closely to their body. These birds need adequate shelter during winter, as their feathers do not provide enough insulation to keep them warm.

▼ *Chicken is one of the most commonly used meats in the world and most parts of the bird can be used as food*

Roman Dorkings

It is believed that the dorking breed of chicken was originally bred in Italy during the reign of Julius Caesar. It was later introduced to England, where the breed was reared commercially. It is considered to be the purest breed because of the five claws on its foot, rather than the usual four. The dorking chicken is a very hardy bird and is extremely active, requiring plenty of space to roam. It is reared both for its meat and eggs and is known to lay eggs in the early part of the year. This bird takes up to two years to grow to a size suitable to eat and can live up to seven years of age. It needs to be given good quality feed to achieve a good weight and size.

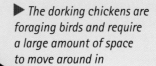

▶ *The dorking chickens are foraging birds and require a large amount of space to move around in*

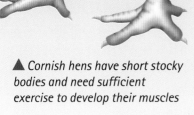

▲ *Cornish hens have short stocky bodies and need sufficient exercise to develop their muscles*

CREATURE PROFILE

Common Name:	Dorking
Colour:	Silver–grey, dark red or white
Weight:	Male: 4 kg (9 lbs)
	Female: 2.7 kg (6 lbs)
Feed on:	Grain, grass and insects

TURKEYS

The turkey is a large bird, found originally in the forests of North America. Today it is bred commercially on farms around the world and is best associated with Christmas celebrations.

Turkey Types

There are two main species of turkeys – the Wild turkey and the Ocellated turkey. Wild turkeys are good fliers and also relatively cunning birds. They are identified by an almost featherless bluish head with a striking red throat in the males. The head also has fleshy growths called caruncles. Wild turkeys live in woodland, where their extremely sharp eyesight allows them to spot danger and adopt a quick means of escape. In the wild, turkeys may nest at the base of a tree during the day, but by night they move higher up and roost in the branches.

◀ *Wild turkeys have a very striking appearance with a particularly dense plumage*

Turkey Treat

The domesticated turkey is raised commercially for its meat and is a descendant of the wild turkey. It is reared extensively in temperate parts of the world. Modern techniques in farming, coupled with a high seasonal demand, have made turkey farming a large-scale operation; the bird is most commonly associated with Christmas celebrations as being a bird large enough to feed gathered families. The most widely-bred variety of domesticated turkey is the broad-breasted white, which is known for its high yield of breast meat, but is said by some to hold less flavour as a result.

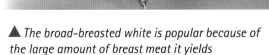

▲ The broad-breasted white is popular because of the large amount of breast meat it yields

CREATURE PROFILE

Common Name:	White midget
Colour:	White with red head and neck
Weight:	Male: 8.2–9 kg (18–20 lbs)
	Female: 4.5–5.4 kg (10–12 lbs)
Feed on:	Grains, plants, seeds and insects

Raising Turkeys

Traditionally, turkeys were bred for their meat during Christmas. Now, they are produced through the year on a large scale. They are reared in large sheds or in barns. Turkeys reared for meat are usually hatched by artificial means. Most commonly turkey hens are now artificially inseminated to fertilise their eggs, as the physical development of male turkeys largely makes them incapable of breeding.

▲ Using artificial incubators to hatch eggs allows breeders to control the number of birds and rear them according to demand

DUCKS

Ducks are common water birds. Many species of ducks are raised on farms for eggs, meat and their soft feathers. Most domestic species of ducks have been bred from the wild Mallard duck.

Pekin Duck

Donald duck, the famous fictional character, is a pekin duck. The classic white pekin duck is a very popular duck breed on farms. It is quite hardy and has a mild temperament and is easy to train, domesticate and pet. It is a fast growing duck and also an excellent egg-layer, laying up to 200 eggs a year. But female pekin ducks are not good brooders, so the eggs usually need to be incubated artificially. The pekin duck is very popular as a meat duck. Adult pekin ducks are white in colour and have orange-yellow bills, legs and feet. The hatchlings have bright yellow-coloured plumage with orange feet.

Rouen Duck

The rouen closely resembles its ancestor, the wild mallard. It is marked with similar colour patterns with a green head, white collar, claret breast and bright-blue feathers on its wings. It is a heavy duck and can weigh up to 5.5 kg (12 lbs). It is not a good egg-layer, typically laying only 100 eggs a year. However, it does yield a good quantity of meat known for its great flavour and is popular for this across Europe. It is used mainy as a roasting duck.

◀ Unlike the brightly-coloured male rouen, the female is distinguished by warm brown colours

Muscovy

The muscovy is another large farm duck. It is the only domestic duck that has not been bred from the mallard duck. It has a bright red crest around its eyes, above the beak. Its feet are equipped with strong and sharp claws that help the bird to roost. It prefers to fly rather than swim. These birds are average egg layers, laying about 80-90 eggs every year. Their meat is leaner than most breeds of duck.

CREATURE PROFILE

Common Name:	Pekin duck
Colour:	White
Weight:	3.5-5 kg (8-11 lbs)
Length:	About 75 cm (30 in)
Feed on:	Insects, grasses and plants

▲ The muscovy duck has a dark coloured body with white wings and long talons on its feet

▼ The pekin duck has relatively weak legs and feet meaning it prefers to swim rather than walk around the farm

OTHER LIVESTOCK

Apart from cattle, horses, sheep, pigs and poultry, some farms also rear more unusual animals like elk, llama, bison and ostrich for commercial purposes; their meat and other products are becoming increasingly accepted.

Elk

The elk is a member of the deer family. It is bred mainly for its antlers and also for game hunting. The antlers of the elk are used to make medicines in South Korea. The male elk has antlers, which are shed every year. The weight of the antlers increases year on year: a one-year-old elk's antlers typically weigh 1.3 kg (2.8 lbs), while a full-grown adult's might weigh up to 11kg (24 lbs).

▼ Alpacas are social animals and live in herds usually at higher altitudes

◀ The elk is the second largest species of deer in the world

Llama and Alpaca

The llama and alpaca both belong to the camel family. The llama resembles a camel but lacks a hump while the alpaca looks like a large sheep. The llama often serves as a beast of burden in some parts of the world, carrying loads from one place to another, especially in hilly areas. Its thick and leathery hoof pads help it get a grip of the rocky surface where most other animals would stumble. The alpaca is bred for its fine wool. Its fleece produces wool, which is much softer and lighter than the wool obtained from sheep. Moreover, the alpaca yields white wool, which is easy to dye in various shades.

CREATURE PROFILE

Common name:	Llama
Colour:	Creamy-white, grey, brown, red or black, or a combination thereof
Height:	1.6–1.8 m (5.5–6 ft) at the shoulder
Weight:	102–204 kg (225–450 lbs)
Feed on:	Shrubs, grass, leaves, lichen

Ostrich

The first South African ostrich farm was founded in 1838. Today ostrich farming is a very profitable enterprise. Most ostrich farms are found in South Africa even today. The ostriches are bred and raised commercially for their meat, skin and feathers. Ostriches yield red meat that tastes like beef and is a delicacy among food lovers. Ostrich leather is very soft and is used to make shoes and bags. The feathers are used to clean fine machinery and even as fashion accessories.

▼ *Ostrich meat is slowly gaining popularity in the world because it is low in fat and cholesterol*

TAKING CARE

Animals at the farm need proper feed, care and medication to stay healthy. Every animal has a different diet and needs to be taken care of differently. So farmers have to be alert about each of their needs.

Food and Shelter

Animals like cows, horses, goats and sheep are all plant eaters but they eat different kinds of plants. The diet of particular animals can depend on the work they do on the farm. Draught horses need more concentrates than the amount needed for cows. Pregnant animals also need a special diet to produce healthy babies. Animals like cows, horses and goats are kept in barns or stables while pigs and sheep are sometimes kept in pens. Farmers must ensure that the barns and pens are spacious, airy, safe and clean. This will help the farm animals stay healthy and happy.

▶ *In many parts of the world there are strict guidelines governing how animals are transported*

Handling Tricks

Handling facilities for cattle and other farm animals do not have to be elaborate and expensive but should be safe and well-controlled. Regular cleaning and maintenance of all kinds of equipment used at the farm is important to avoid any chance of disease or infection. Cattle sorting, loading and transporting is a very important aspect of commercial farming. All vehicles used should have a proper flooring, solid latches and adequate ventilation to allow the animals to move about and breathe freely in the vehicle during transportation.

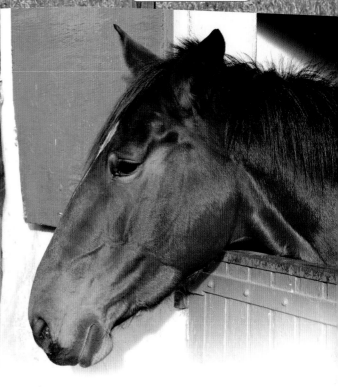

▲ Stables and barns need to be kept clean to avoid disease and infection

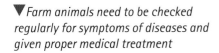

▼ Farm animals need to be checked regularly for symptoms of diseases and given proper medical treatment

Disease and Cure

Animals at the farm are prone to illness. Because many animals live together on farms in concentration, the threat of infections spreading is a real and present danger: flu is a common threat to many farm animals; bluetongue, a viral disease in cattle, goats and sheep causes inflammation and swelling of mouth, nose and tongue and can be fatal if not treated; cloven-hooved animals are at partical risk of foot problems and must be shoed regularly to avoid diseases like laminitis and even lameness. Hygienic conditions and healthy living help prevent diseases.

▲ Poultry coops should be clean, hygienic and safe from predators and other farm animals

POULTRY CARE

The health of poultry affects their eggs and meat, so proper feed and medication is important. Poultry also face the threat of predation from other animals, so measures need to be taken for their protection.

Home Sweet Home

Having clean and safe housing for poultry is of the utmost importance. Some farms let their poultry run free. This gives the poultry freedom but might be dangerous and lead to accidents and fatalities. Farms can also opt for a bottomless poultry coop which can be transferred from one place to the other on the farm; this keeps them safe while allowing them enough freedom to move within the coop. Poultry coops do not need to be very elaborate but should fulfill basic requirements by providing proper ventilation and shelter.

Caring for the Young

Looking after young chicks and ducklings is a very important part of poultry care. Both the young and the parent need to be provided food and water separately. Often the mother breaks the grain into smaller pieces in order to feed her young. The food should be in a container that cannot be tipped over by the chicks or ducklings while feeding. The water should also be kept in a shallow container so that the chicks do not drown. The young birds should be moved to a larger rearing coop when they are about 8 weeks of age.

Common Diseases

Bird flu is a common yet potentially dangerous disease. Not only does it spread rapidly, but, if not detected properly it can also affect the health of anybody who might eat the meat. Precaution and medical attention can, however, reduce its threat. Fowl cholera, fowl typhoid and fowl pox are other common diseases in poultry. Most of these diseases can be prevented by a healthy diet. Poultry feed should ideally contain 20-22 per cent of proteins with coccodiostat, a chemical that helps to build immunity. Cleanliness and hygiene also helps prevent most poultry diseases.

▼ For the first weeks after birth, the chicks should be kept with their parent

▲ All poultry should be given a separate place and dish for their food and water and the parent and young should be fed separately

FARM STORIES

Farm animals have long been a favourite with storytellers. They are portrayed as friendly creatures in most children's books. The farm has also been used to symbolise human society; this is known as an *allegory*.

Old McDonald

One of the strongest fictional associations with farms is the character Old McDonald, immortalised in the famous nursery rhyme. The song introduces the various animals found at the farm, therefore helping little children learn their names. It also helps children learn the different sounds that each of the farm animals make – from mooing cows to quacking ducks.

▶ *The Old McDonald nursery rhyme is an enduring favourite with children and teaches them about farm animals and their calls*

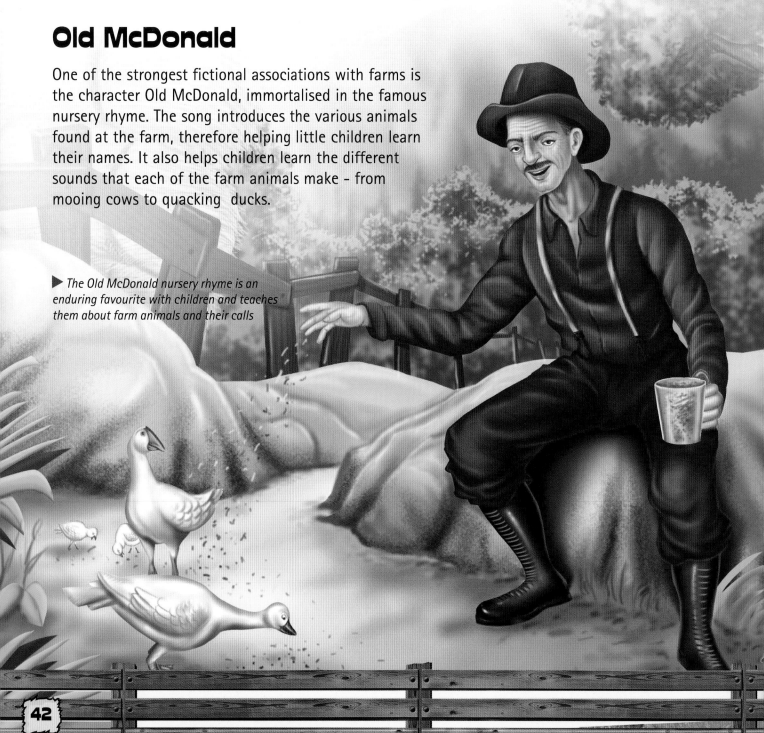

Old, Old Tales

Farm animals are often used in stories to give moral lessons. Aesop, a storyteller, who lived in ancient Greece around the 6th century B.C., wrote several tales about animals to teach right and wrong behaviour; for example, his story of the goose that laid golden eggs is a lesson for the greedy; it narrates the story of a couple who had a goose which laid a golden egg every day. The couple got greedy and killed the goose one day in order to possess all the gold at once. But they were left with nothing!

▼ Aesop's Fables makes use of various animals teach moral lessons

Animal Farm

More recently, George Orwell wrote Animal Farm, in which the farm and farm animals represented world politics and political figures. The main characters of the novel are farm animals like pigs, horses, donkeys and goats. They manage to overthrow human beings from the farm. They begin ruling the farm with the idea of being better and fairer than humans. But they too end up being as corrupt. The novel cleverly refers to real political incidents like the Russian Revolution and famous politicians like Stalin and Lenin, with the aim of ridiculing them - a technique known as satirical allegory.

◄ George Orwell's Animal Farm has became one of the most important books of his generation

Glossary

Adapt: Make suitable for a new use or purpose

Asset: Something of worth

Agility: Physical and mental speed

Bovine: Family of cows

Bred: Reared

Castrated: Removal of male reproductive organs of animals

Cautious: Careful

Compatible: Easy to mix with

Crest: Crown

Docile: Timid

Domesticate: To bring animals under human control

Draught animals: Animals used for pulling heavy loads

Endurance: Ability to work longer

Foal: Young horse

Harness: To hold something in place with straps

Hygienic: Clean

Incubate: Keeping eggs warm to allow them to hatch better

Insulation: Protection from cold

Invaluable: Precious

Malnourished: In bad health due to lack of food

Nutritious: Healthy

Paddock: A small field where horses are kept

Resistant: Against

Sage: A kind of herb

Stamina: Energy

Sturdier: Stronger

Thrifty: Avoiding waste

Weaning: Moving a baby from mother's milk to solid food

Westward migration: The migration of a large number of people mainly from Europe to American states like Ohio, Tennessee and Kentucky.

Yield: Given amount

Index

A
Aesop 43
Alpaca 36
Angora 21
Angus cattle 12
Animal Farm 43
Antlers 36, 38, 44
Australian cattle dog 28, 29
Ayrshire 16, 17

B
Bison 36, 45
Blade shear 24
Bluetongue 39
Border collie 29
Breeding 6, 7, 26, 44
Broad-breasted White turkey 33
Buck 20

Bull trains 17
Butterfat 13, 14

C
Caruncles 32
Cashmere 21
Coccodiostat 41
Cornish hen 30, 31
Cornwall 30
Coyotes 24

D
Devon pig 27
Domestic pig 27
Domesticated 10, 20, 24, 30, 33
Donald duck 34
Dorking breed 31
Draught 16, 17, 18, 19, 38
Drip water systems 26

E
East Friesian 25
Elk 36

F
Fowl cholera 41
Fowl typhoid 41
Fowl 30, 41

G
George Orwell 43
Ghee 14

H
Heelers 28
Herding dogs 28
Holstein 12, 13, 15

Immunity 41
Irish draught Horse 19

J
Jersey 13
Julius Caesar 31

L
Laminitis 39
large black pig 27
Livestock 5, 8, 9, 36, 44

llama 36, 37

M
Machine shear 24
Mallard duck 34, 35
Miniature Mediterranean donkey 22
Mozzarella 15
Mule 22
Murrah 15
Muscovy 35

O
Ocellated turkey 32
Old McDonald 42
Ostrich 36, 37
Oxen 5, 6, 16, 17

P
Paddock 24
Pekin duck 34, 35
Piggeries 26
Pullets 30

Q
Queensland heeler 29